HELL NO!
I am Not Black,
and
You are Not White

Hell No to Crime

Admire T. Kadenge

Bloomington, IN  Milton Keynes, UK

AuthorHouse™
1663 Liberty Drive, Suite 200
Bloomington, IN 47403
www.authorhouse.com
Phone: 1-800-839-8640

AuthorHouse™ UK Ltd.
500 Avebury Boulevard
Central Milton Keynes, MK9 2BE
www.authorhouse.co.uk
Phone: 08001974150

First published by AuthorHouse 10/4/2006

ISBN: 1-4208-7660-0 (sc)

Printed in the United States of America
Bloomington, Indiana

This book is printed on acid-free paper.

"Edited By Arabla Welbeck"

Contents

Introduction

I am troubled by the different versions of racism in America. The struggle to end racism continues today and I am adding my efforts to it. I have joined in the discussion to end it. I have written this book in acknowledgement of all who have paved the way before me to grant me the freedom to write. I am acknowledging their sacrifices and hard work in the different areas of their achievements in the civil rights movements. So many of them lost their lives. Others are not even recognized in history books. I am thankful for their lives.

It is certainly not possible to discuss all the different facets of racism that exist today or those that I have personally observed or even experienced. I plan to concentrate only on one area that is taken for granted and that has often been overlooked. It is the use of the words "Black" and "White" as racial classifications for people of African and European origin respectively.

In discussing my concerns, I will base my opinions on the universally recognized Webster's Dictionary, specifically the Merriam Webster's Collegiate Dictionary, Tenth Edition. The Webster's Dictionary is one of the most popular dictionaries of today and is respected and authorized to be used in schools to educate our children by providing definitions of the English language worldwide. If I accomplish my task, you should be able to join me in proclaiming, "Hell No! I am not Black and you are not White" or "I am not White and you are not Black", as the case maybe.

CHAPTER 1

I was born in Zimbabwe. My parents, grand parents and great grand parents were all born in southern Africa. We all did not have any inter-racial marriages. My race is African. IT IS NOT BLACK. The dictionary's most accurate definition of "race" for my topic of discussion, which is racial classification, is "a division of mankind possessing traits that are transmissible by descent and sufficient to characterize it as a distinct human type". The Merriam Webster's Collegiate Dictionary only defines African as:

1. A native or inhabitant of Africa

2.   A person, and especially a BLACK person of immediate or remote African ancestry

The dictionary fails to define or classify "African" as a RACE of people originating from Africa.

I was blessed to come to America decades ago. Since then, I have filled out application forms in schools and places of employment, as well as different types of legal paperwork. As I filled out these forms, I was required to provide my racial identity. Whilst providing my racial identity to colleges and employers, I had to unwillingly check "Black" as being my race. There were spaces to check for the different races such as White, Black, Hispanic, Asian etc. Some documents did provide a space to specify "other". Therefore asking me to identify my race as "Black" at that time was and is still a standard practice.

As time passed I started to understand the problems and frustrations these classifications were raising. Most of the problems stemmed from the misrepresentations of racial classification. For some reason Africans, African-Americans and other members of the African Diaspora had come to accept the label "Black".

Below are issues raised by some African-Americans as well as some general concerns I encountered before writing this book.

1. *Why was a person's race called African when he was born in the United States and he had mixed racial traits and characteristics from other races?*

2. *Why did some African-Americans still call themselves "Niggers"?*

3. *Some African-Americans did not want to be called Africans or African-Americans. They preferred to be called Blacks or Black Americans. They did not want to be connected to Africa, because Africa was plagued with problems they did not wish to be associated with.*

4. *Some African-Americans preferred to just be called American. They were however troubled by*

the discrimination they experienced because of their complexion.

5. Some did not care what they were called; they accepted any classification they were given.

6. Some preferred to call themselves Africans or African-Americans. This group however was under the impression that Africans from Africa or Africans in Africa would not accept them knowing that they had been estranged from Africa and could not speak African languages, not to mention the apparent differences in their physical traits.

7. Some people accepted to be called "Black" because it was an official classification they had known all their lives through governmental documentation, the educational system and civil rights battles that exposed "Nigger" as an offensive word.

8. Some older African-Americans still called themselves "Colored" or "People of Color".

9. Very few European-Americans called themselves by their respective geographical country of origin, for example, Russian-American, French-American, Italian-American, British-American

etc. Most Europeans and European-Americans called themselves "White". Very few called themselves "Caucasians", which is a more appropriate classification.

In my opinion, it is wrong to use "Black" or "White" as racial classifications regardless of the reasons. This type of classification is a product of the past. It did not just originate out of the blue to become the standard that it is today. It is important to study its history in order to understand how it came about. I have consulted the Webster's Dictionary. I believe the authors may have undertaken extensive research and done a historical background check in order to provide definitions.

CHAPTER 2

The Webster's Dictionary describes "Black" in a way I feel is wrong. The dictionary has many definitions of the word black. Most of them have negative meanings. One definition indirectly connects the word black to Africans and descendants of Africans by defining black as "a person belonging to any of various population groups having dark pigmentation of the skin". In this definition of black, the dictionary does not directly connect the word black to Africans. Yet, in the definition of African ("a person and especially a black person of immediate or remote African ancestry"), it directly connects the word African to a black person.

The dictionary also does not directly connect the definition of Black to Nigger, Negroid, Negress etc., though the same dictionary describes these very words to mean a "Black" person.

It defines Nigger as:

1. *A black person – usually taken to be offensive*
2. *A member of any dark-skinned race – usually taken to be offensive*
3. *A member of any socially disadvantaged class of persons*

According to the dictionary a nigger is a black person. ***THEREFORE BEING CALLED BLACK WOULD BE JUST THE SAME AS BEING CALLED NIGGER, WHICH IS OFFENSIVE.***

With such disconnected descriptions and definitions of African, Black and Nigger, no wonder the public has not been able to decipher the offensiveness of Black as a racial classification. It is time to reject it publicly and officially.

In my opinion, the present use of this word "Black" in official documents and in different organizations was not intended to offend anyone. It was merely done to identify the racial make-up of the descendants of Africans to avoid racial discrimination in the educational system and employment. This was initiated after the abolition of slavery through the legislation of civil rights laws created by the civil rights movement.

Why does the Webster's Dictionary define "Nigger" as "a member of a socially disadvantaged class of persons"? A MEMBER OF A SOCIALLY DISADVANTAGED CLASS OF PERSONS INDEED! Persons of all races may fall under this category.

Why did the Merriam Webster's Collegiate Dictionary label only people of African origin as socially disadvantaged? By the dictionary's definition, would a socially disadvantaged Caucasian be a nigger too?

I bet not!

This shows that we should not always trust the Webster's Dictionary to protect our identity and that of our children (who are educated from the same dictionary) by correctly defining who we are. We should not expect the dictionary to protect us from the jaws of racism or to teach us everything we need to know, at least about ourselves.

The dictionary is protected by the First Amendment and thus it can say whatever it wants to. But I am challenging it now. The dictionary does not have a logical reason to call my race Black. It is called African. Globally, we need to replace the racial classification of "Black" for native Africans and Africans in the Diaspora with a label that better describes them.

My racial name as described in the Webster's Dictionary was imposed by the English language without any authority from the actual people concerned. The Webster's Dictionary was written to represent the English language, which belongs to the British and their descendants only. Their definitions of other races are based on their history of colonialism without respect for the views of the native people involved.

CHAPTER 3

Within schools, churches, courts, governmental organizations, the media and the general public, the word "black" is so deeply rooted that people use it casually. Should you ask any member of the groups mentioned above if he or she is aware that using the word "black" is just as offensive as using the word "nigger", he or she would most likely say no. For generations, no one took the time and steps to isolate the word and expose its true meaning.

How did the use of the word black come to signify the African race? The Mcrriam Webster's Collegiate Dictionary defines the word "nigger" as "a black person ..." In its definition, the dictionary informs that the word "nigger" was derived from an earlier word "neger", which was derived from the French word "negre". The word "negre" came from the Spanish or Portuguese word "negro", which simply means the color black. The Portuguese, the Spanish and the French had attempted to describe the color of the skin and did not use the word black as a racial classification. Who in the world twisted the term for the color black to signify the entire race of people of African origin?

We all know that the complexion of the majority of Africans is not black. From Egypt all the way down to South Africa, there are different complexions that do not come close to being black at all. Again, my point is, if the dictionary wants to identify people by the color of their skin, it should do so without letting it signify a race. Moreover, if the Webster's Dictionary wants to classify people by their skin color, it should state what the true color is.

Most African people's complexion is not black and that of European people is not white. To further understand the meaning of both Black and White, let us research how both words are used in the dictionary. In looking at the way the Webster's Dictionary describes "black", one wonders how a color description could be loaded with so much negativity, such as:

1. *thoroughly sinister or evil*
2. *wicked*
3. *indicative of condemnation or discredit*
4. *connected with or invoking the supernatural and especially the devil*

Why would anyone choose to use a word that is so negative to describe the race of another human being? What did they aim to achieve?

Other descriptions are:

5. *marked by the occurrence of disaster*
6. *very sad, gloomy or calamitous*
7. *characterized by hostility or angry discontent*
8. *a refusal to be sociable*

9. *characterized by grim, distorted or grotesque satire*

If a child of African descent who is eager to learn about his race picks up the dictionary and finds Black inscribed in such derogatory and dehumanizing descriptions, he is bound to be hurt, disappointed and saddened if not ashamed of his race. Will this child be proud of his race? He will more likely say, "I do not want to be Black". If he then reads the definition of White, only to find positive definitions, why would he not want to be White instead of Black?

We as human beings should carefully choose the words we use in our different languages in order not to hurt, harm or belittle other people. Words are very powerful in that what we speak or pronounce on others can become a reality. This is why when we name our children or each other, we should use positive names. It is wrong to use negative words to name ourselves or use negative racial names on other races.

When we find such words, we should be willing to isolate and condemn them in order to create a harmonious integrated society that we all want to live in. Our willingness to change when we discover the use of harmful negatively loaded words in the different languages we speak should be viewed positively as a step forward to true racial integration.

Society's failure to use proper descriptive racial classifications, as noted above, bears serious consequences. Improper racial classifications may lead to social ills such as gangs, racial hatred, discrimination, segregation and apartheid behaviors. In the United States, one of the major problems we have is gang explosion. Gangs from the African-American, Hispanic-American, Asian-American and European-American communities (White supremacist groups) are arising from racial misconceptions and social ills as discussed above. All gangs are dangerous regardless of origin, racial make up or level of complexity.

In the African-American communities many of the causes of gangs could relate to the negative depiction of black and its use as a racial classification. A child who reads the dictionary and finds discouraging descriptions of his race as Black may think, "I am black and therefore I am supposed to be wicked, evil, thoroughly sinister, hostile, etc. I cannot amount to anything good." Any of the nine descriptions mentioned above could attribute to this mindset.

History highlights prime examples of the consequences of these definitions. If you study history you will find examples of racist remarks and policies that reinforced the negative use of Black towards people of African origin. There was a time when it was legal to discriminate and dehumanize people of African origin. The programming of the negatives associated with Black was done legally. For so long there was little success in challenging that kind of programming. Then came substantial resistances and struggles for civil rights which produced many positive changes. After that there has not been sufficient analytical outcry challenging Black itself as a racial classification.

We will now examine the Webster's Dictionary's definition of white. The descriptions in the definitions do not surprise me since we have been programmed to register white as the opposite of black. The dictionary contains only positive definitions of white. The definitions are:

1. *a. free from color*
   b. of the color of new snow or milk; specifically of the color white
   c. light or pallid in color
   d. lustrous pale gray; silvery; made of silver
2. *a. being a member of a group or race characterized by reduced pigmentation and usually specifically distinguished from persons belonging to groups marked by black, brown, yellow, or red skin coloration*
   b. of, relating to, characteristic of, or consisting of white people

   c. *marked upright fairness*

3. *free from spot or blemish; as:*

   a. *free from moral impurity: INNOCENT: marked by the wearing of white by a woman as a symbol of purity*

   b. *not intended to cause harm*

   c. *favorable, fortunate*

4. *a person belonging to a light-skinned race*

With descriptions like these noted above, who would not want to be associated with this "White" race? Is it any wonder that the authors of the Webster's Dictionary associate these definitions with the European race? In looking at the positive definitions of white, do you not wonder why the authors (or whoever chose these words originally) did not pick similar positive descriptions for people of African origin? When a child of European origin reads this and relates it to his race, would that not make him proud? He might question the "free from color" definition since there is no complexion that is free from color. Otherwise everything else is fine.

Note how the authors took the time to point out the differences between Caucasians ("Whites") and people of other races. One definition of white states, "being a member of a group or race characterized by reduced pigmentation and usually specifically distinguished from persons belonging to groups marked by black, brown, yellow, or red skin coloration". Another definition states, "a person belonging to a light-skinned race". What do they mean by light-skinned? Are Japanese people white too? They are light-skinned when compared to Indians, who in turn are light-skinned when compared to some Africans.

The dictionary has so much disregard for African people and people of African descent. Only under the definition of Negro does it come out to say "black" is a race. First, it defines Negro as:

"a member of the ***black race*** distinguished from members of other races by usually inherited physical and physiological characteristics without regard to language or culture; especially: a member of a people belonging to the <u>African branch of the black race</u> – sometimes taken to be offensive"

Secondly, what does *"African branch of the black race"* mean? Do the dictionary's authors mean "African" originated from " the black race"? Do they not understand that "African" is the race of all people of African origin, be they native Africans or descendants of Africans? African is the parent channel.

Why did the dictionary fail to indicate black as a race under the very definition of black? The Merriam Webster's Collegiate Dictionary's definition of a "black" person is "a person belonging to any of various population *groups* having dark pigmentation of the skin." The dictionary does not even define "black" as a race under the definitions it provides for black. Yet under the definition of white it recognizes a "white" person as " a member of a group or *race*" in comparison to " persons belonging to *groups* marked by black, brown, yellow, or red skin coloration".

Note the dictionary's definition of white in:

(a) being a member of a group characterized by reduced pigmentation and usually specifically distinguished from persons belonging to groups marked by black, brown, yellow, or red skin coloration

(b) *of, relating to, characteristic of, or consisting of white people*

followed directly and so tactfully by

(c) marked upright fairness

Recognize the use of the word "marked", followed by a positive description in "marked upright fairness". Another definition of white states "free from spot or blemish: as free from moral impurity: innocent".

Why then does the same dictionary, after it has provided definitions of a "black" person, provide negative definitions like "dirty, soiled", "thoroughly sinister or evil: wicked", "indicative of condemnation or

23

discredit", "connected with or invoking the supernatural and especially the devil" and "marked by the occurrence of disaster"? Why link the devil to a word that also describes a person's race? For God's sake, why that implication?

Who was it that originally thought of linking the words black and white to race? It seems to me that there was a conscious effort or a plot to establish a system of supremacy of Caucasians ("white") over all African people ("blacks"). I can assure you that if Africans had written the dictionary, they would not have demoralized another race as seen in this dictionary. It is insensitive, harmful, offensive and purely racist.

Nobody ever calls supposed 'yellow-skinned' people (as the dictionary suggests in "persons belonging to groups marked by black, brown, yellow, or red skin coloration") *yellow people*. Nobody ever calls someone a red person, a brown person etc. Why do we then call

Caucasians "white" people and people of African origin "black" people?

There is a great need for bold, painful, leadership-oriented changes in "black" and "white" racial classifications in order to achieve true harmony. If humanity wants equality and harmony in this world, we must change the way we define or name ourselves. This should start in the family unit and progress through communities, local governments, state and federal levels, nationally and internationally. Humanity must demand this.

Governments must not be blamed for requiring racial information on official documents. The request for racial classifications on official documents is not wrong. If there were no classifications, the government would have no way of identifying and helping the minorities of this country. America must eliminate the offensive racial classification of "black" entirely, in spoken and written language, and replace it with

"African-American" , "descendant of Africa" or "of African descent".

I am not challenging the official document format mentioned above. I am merely challenging the wording. Again, there is nothing wrong with the request for racial information in itself. We must not forget that this information is crucial in the allocation and distribution of monies from the different government, social and educational funds available for providing resources and services needed by the public. To a large extent this information protects minorities from discrimination or exclusion from services due them.

It may be argued too that this information could expose minorities to potential discrimination in job hiring, and in the allocation of goods and services. Those who discriminate will do so anyway regardless of the illegalities, but it is still very important for governmental agencies to know the makeup of all the different races in government, private and educational institutions. This is accomplished by asking the public to identify their race.

CHAPTER 4

At the time the decision was made to classify people as Blacks or Whites, no one successfully protested that this labeling was wrong. Had somebody raised the issue about these labels, which would have resulted in the proper naming of the classifications, I would not have been writing about it now. Since there was no outcry over these labels, America and the rest of the world are still struggling to control the racial hostilities that stem from these classifications.

Those who could have questioned the labels did not focus their attention on the negative connotations of Black, not only Nigger, as compared to White. They simply did not realize the derogatory meaning of the label black. Otherwise they would not have embraced that sinister label. Practically everyone knew and still knows that the use of the word Nigger is an offensive racial classification. As a result of the negative connotations in the definition of Black, Black should also be considered as offensive and placed in the same category as Nigger.

To analyze this we could use the rules of arithmetic. Take the equation 2+3=5. Two plus three will always be equal to five. Each side of the equation holds true. You cannot accept the validity of the right side and reject the left side, or vice versa. One side of an equation must be equal to the other. Black and Nigger are both condescending.

I can imagine that one of the reasons no one rose up to question the classification labels was because the majority of people were satisfied with the enacted civil rights legislation of their time.

After the civil rights gains mentioned above, Africans and African-Americans did not challenge the label of black as a racial classification. People may have looked at the skin color of an African or African-American and accepted it as being close enough to black and thus settled for that label.

It could also be that they did not push the envelope further because the struggle for civil rights had been long, deadly and tiring. These were major accomplishments on their own over which great leaders such as Dr. Martin Luther King Jr., Rosa Parks and others risked their lives. Much as current leaders like the Rev. Jesse Jackson and the Rev. Al Sharpton and others are doing today, past civil rights leaders worked positively to curb racial injustices; and some of them did so even to the point of losing their lives.

During the Selma-to-Montgomery March for voting rights on Bloody Sunday March 7, 1965, for example, many people lost their lives. In Selma, Alabama, you will find the following martyrs listed at the memorial: Jimmy Lee Jackson (1938-1965), Viola Gregg Liuzzo (1925-1965), Rev. James Reeb (1927-1965), Jonathan

Daniels (1939-1965), Medgar Evers, Michael Schwerner, James Chaney, Andrew Goodman and Sammy Young, Jr. They must not be forgotten. They must be honored and remembered. Their efforts led to the signing of the Voting Rights Act of 1965 by President Lyndon Baines Johnson.

Under the National Trail System Act of 1968, Congress created the Selma-to-Montgomery National Trail in 1996 to commemorate the significance of the March in American history. We could at least maintain the memorial that was built at the Selma-to-Montgomery National Historic Trail in Selma, Alabama and the trail itself so that they would not lie in the state of deterioration in which they are found today.

The United States Congress and people of African descent need to step up in our communities to raise the required funds to maintain this memorial and trail. We must not forsake these sites. We must visit them. As we do so we will educate our families about the lives that were lost and the sacrifices this nation's people went through to obtain the rights we now take for granted.

As time passed, civil rights leaders initiated the use of Afro-American rather than the label Black. This occurred with the onset of Alex Haley's book ROOTS from which the television miniseries ROOTS was derived. The realization set in that the connection to their African ancestry was a right, and not a choice. That realization brought on a push to be classified as Afro-American rather than just Black.

The classification has now been upgraded to African-American. However, the push has not been strong enough to bring about significant changes to eliminate "Black" as a racial classification entirely. Moreover, Africans and their descendents did not institute the classification of Black as identification for the African race. The Europeans did.

At the time of the Civil Rights struggle, African-Americans were referred to as Negroes in addition to more condescending labels like Colored, Nigger or Boy. There was no awareness that Negro in itself (which is the Spanish word for the color black) was a racist classification.

The amount of energy that went into the Civil Rights Movement and the efforts required to pass those laws were great achievements. As commented before, the monumental events must have drained the participants of the different civil rights movements such as civil rights groups and their leaders, the US congress and respective presidents.

The general movement was supposed to have ended discrimination in the United States, which did not happen. To this day there are people who still claim that there is no discrimination in this country. I have heard this assertion mainly from the European-American communities.

There are some who think that complaints about racism that most Africans and African-Americans raise are unfounded. An everyday occurrence is when African-Americans are denied employment based on their names and not the qualifications cited on job applications.

Such discrimination may be enhanced by the call out for their racial classification on job application forms, which reveals their racial identity outright. The presence of racial classification on a job application is required by the government to identify and ensure the employment of minorities. If the government relaxes this enforcement, the public will be free to openly discriminate.

There are other examples of discrimination that involve the justice system, educational institutions and the private sector whereby a person is misjudged at trial, denied access to quality education and treated unfairly just because of his race. For example, why is there a higher percentage of African-Americans among prisoners incarcerated today? Why is there a lower percentage of minorities in colleges? Why are there fewer minorities in management levels in most companies? This cannot be the objective, orchestration or desire of the government.

It is unfortunate that government resources for the enforcement of civil rights are spread too thin. The public is not willing to pay more taxes for the sole purpose of enforcing compliance to civil rights laws. Would it then be willing to deal with the additional concern of Africans and African-Americans not wanting to be labeled "Black"?

Why does this concern me so much? My concern, though personal, is valid. I am addressing a subject that I feel is not getting the attention it deserves. It affects people of all races. It can help build racial harmony in communities that are struggling with race issues by finding a common ground between different racial groups. It can produce or reinforce significant trust among people of all races. It can make all people proud of their race. It can stop some of the racial hostilities we see today.

I could go on and on with the advantages and positive changes this could bring. Let me repeat what I said earlier that my discussion of the subject in this book can best be reviewed using the facts found in an independent book, The Merriam Webster's Collegiate Dictionary, Tenth Edition. Almost everybody is familiar with the Webster's Dictionary. It is readily available in local libraries.

In order to review and evaluate this discussion fairly, you may start by analyzing it the way I did using the dictionary. You can start by looking for the definitions of Black, race, and White. From these words, you will find other keywords that are used in the definitions. The point of looking up words in a dictionary is as follows.

The dictionary is expected to give you as accurate a definition in that language as possible because the authors do their research thoroughly before writing it. They reflect the substance of the meaning of the words as closely as possible to the real or original meaning so that the words can be best understood.

Therefore, by using the dictionary I am confident that I am extremely close to the true meaning of the word I am researching. If I am not, at least I know I have tried to understand a language which, in this case, is not my own or my mother tongue. For the purpose of discussing this topic of racial classification, the dictionary is my first choice. This is because the dictionary should be the foundation of language. It should be doing a better job of defining the language. I do not agree with its definitions of Black and White as racial classifications.

In order to draw your own conclusion, you may look up the following words and phrases in the dictionary. They are: family, people, breeding stock (which in the Merriam Webster's Collegiate Dictionary, Tenth Edition, appears in the definition of race), tribe, class, kind, species, traits, distinct human type (which also appears in the definition of race), ancestry, Nigger,

Negro, Negroid, Negress, Negrillo, Negritto, Africa, color, sullen, pallid, and Caucasian.

With the phrases, isolate the words first. After you have isolated the words, find their meanings so that the total meaning can be made clear to you before you conclude.

CHAPTER 5

There are many definitions in the dictionary for the words black and white. I am very concerned about the definitions that are given to both words. Each word has various meanings, depending on how it is used. When the Webster's Dictionary defines the noun Nigger, it points out that it is an offensive term. It describes Nigger, Negro and Negress as Black but does not directly describe Black to mean Nigger, Negro or Negress. I believe that the authors of the Webster's Dictionary knew that directly associating Black with Nigger, Negro or Negress would have openly offended the African and African-American communities. If not, what could have been their logical reason?

I pointed out earlier various definitions of the adjective black. All of those descriptions are negative, offensive, demoralizing and dehumanizing. But when we look at the adjective white, and we follow the same analysis, the dictionary starts by saying, "free from color."

Then all of a sudden, the definition is tied to the color white.

How can something be "free from color" and still have color at the same time? Why the conflict? The color white is then tied to colors that are pallid, gray and silver. From there, the Webster's Dictionary describes a race and takes time to differentiate it from people it had given descriptive complexions of black, brown and yellow. Why?

Why did the Webster's authors have to define the White race by differentiating it from people of other complexions? It seems they were trying to establish some form of supremacy between the races. Is this an attempt to discriminate or separate the "Caucasian race" from any other race?

The dictionary defines Caucasian (adjective) as:

1. *of or relating to the Caucasus or its inhabitants*
2. *a) of or relating to the white race of humankind as classified according to physical features*
   b) of or relating to the white race as defined by law specifically as composed of persons of European, North African, or southwest Asian ancestry

Why should the law play a role in how a dictionary defines a race? Whose law is it anyway?

What does the law have to do with the meaning of race? If the law is involved in determining white racial identity, as the dictionary definition states, why does this rule not also apply in the definitions of the other races?

Where else in the dictionary has any other race apart from the white race been so explicitly classified as "… race of humankind"? Why is there seemingly a motive to elevate the white race above all other races? All races fall under the category "… race of humankind".

In the definition of the adjective white, the meaning is tied to fairness, purity, and innocence, including harmless in "White lie". Are the Webster's authors here implying that there is another kind of lie that is harmful and as a result, the opposite of a white lie? Though the term "Black lie" does not exist, is it surprising that "Black book" and "Black list" for example, do exist?

A lie is a lie and will always be a lie, regardless of whether it is black or white. I do not believe the Webster's authors had any intentions to associate this harmless lie with any of the people of "black, brown, yellow, or red skin coloration" as described in the dictionary. The Webster's authors' use of white as an adjective is quite different from their use of the adjective black.

It seems to me that there was an intent to portray Africans and African-Americans as negatively as possible, while Europeans or Caucasians were portrayed as positive. If I am wrong, then I stand to be corrected.

As you compare the definitions of black and white, try to find some fairness between them and rationalize what meaning was intended. Would it be unfair for me as an African (who I am proud to be, with no apology) to assume that the owners of the English language (represented by the Webster's authors) do not like my race?

Would I be wrong to also assume that the owners of this language wanted to praise their own race while looking down on mine? I do not believe there was any fairness at all. At least, as far as I can see, the dictionary's authors purposely neglected to classify "African" as the race of the African people and concentrated on what the slave owners then or what the Caucasian race preferred to call them. They relied on what the owners of the English language labeled the African people.

If they did not know what race the African people belonged to, they could have just asked. The Africans would have simply told them that racial classification is geographically connected.

Do you believe that the authors of this Tenth Edition of the Merriam Webster's Collegiate Dictionary did not know that "African" was the true race of the people from Africa, including their descendants? They must have known it. We have been programmed to accept classifications like the Asian race and the European race (which pertain to geographic origin). Why not also the African race?

When the dictionary defines the Asian and European races, it does so in connection to the geographic point of origin, that is, the continents of Asia and Europe. It is only in the definition of African that the dictionary attaches skin color to the meaning.

In the definitions of Asian and European the dictionary begins by defining these races in their adjective form. Only in the definition of African does the dictionary begin by defining African as a noun and it is in that definition that it mentions skin color. Let us review the definitions below.

Asian (adjective): of, relating to, or characteristic of the continent of Asia or its people

Asian (noun): a native or inhabitant of Asia

European (adjective): of, relating to, or characteristic of the continent of Europe or its people

European (noun): 1. a native or inhabitant of Europe

2. a person of European descent

African (noun): 1. a native or inhabitant of Africa

2. a person and <u>especially</u> a black person of immediate or remote African ancestry

African (adjective): of, or relating to, or characteristic of the continent of Africa or its people

From the above, the dictionary's authors convey the following in the definition of African as a noun:

A, they are implying that colors and complexions signify a person's race.

B, they are implying that colors and complexions can be interchanged with race.

C, they are implying that words which describe a person's color or complexion can be interchanged with his race.

D, they are equating colors and complexions with race.

Authors who for some reason write while ignoring the existence and contribution of people of other races puzzle me. This practice is not only evident in the dictionary. I see this also in history books where people have written about the discovery of famous land sites or places of interest. For example, historians wrote that David Livingston discovered the Victoria Falls in my country Zimbabwe, as if there were no native people who had been living at the falls for generations.

To be fair to the authors of the Webster's Dictionary, it is probably not their fault that they defined my race as "black". They built their knowledge upon whatever the owners of the English language provided them.

CHAPTER 6

I would not have written this book if I did not expect some participation from you. May you take a more active role in educating yourself, your children and community. I believe I have brought to your attention a subject you can ponder over and care enough about to discuss positively to achieve harmony in our society.

There are some key areas that need to be looked at. One of these is the educational medium as a whole. Dictionaries, which provide word meanings, are critical in the education of our children. They are used in schools as a basis to acquire knowledge. They are an integral part of a child's school curriculum.

If a child takes the dictionary and learns that Black is defined as a race of people that originate from Africa and that the same dictionary provides other definitions of black in negative terms, will he not mentally associate the black race with negativity? In the child's mind, that negative connection of the "Black" race to the other definitions of black must be broken. He must be made to understand that there is no race called "Black", regardless of the connection the dictionary makes.

We have overlooked this foundational racial misrepresentation for generations. This kind of discriminatory classification at the foundational level has produced negative effects on race relations in this country and everywhere else in the world today.

Are there other books in the school curriculum that perpetrate this kind of discrimination? Yes. Though these texts do not directly describe the African people in openly negative terms, they allude to that negativity or imply it. This is evident even in the way we label course titles in college. Until recently, college-level courses on

African-American studies were labeled Black Studies. Take the following hypothetical statement, "Mr. Jones was encouraged by the Black Studies he took at the University of Southern California." The word black in Black Studies would refer to a race.

Why were courses not originally labeled African or African-American Studies? If a school labels some of its courses or departmental studies "black", the students would automatically accept that labeling as a true racial description. If they go against the status quo and reject it, would they not risk being "black listed" (a phrase which connotes negativity, as described by the dictionary)?

How often do we unconsciously use "black" in our everyday lives, like "black market", "black magic", "black history", "black studies" and "black culture"? February is even called "Black History Month". Are we really thinking about the meaning of the word "black"? Surprisingly, these misrepresentations are present in educational and historical books and in everyday communication, the very places they should not be in.

People who were insensitive to African people and their descendants wrote the dictionary. The racial descriptions and classifications that are in the Webster's Dictionary were not fully researched from the African perspective. Africans and their descendants should have been consulted in areas that involved them. And even if they were, who was to determine which areas of interest warranted the input of Africans or the African point of view?

An unbiased and authentic research of African Studies would classify the African race using definitions that make sense and are valid, such as tribal identity, kingdoms and geographical identity, but not color or complexion. The dictionary's descriptions of "tribe" do not reflect the description of tribe as it relates to the African race.

Some of the definitions are:

1 (a) *a social group comprising numerous families, clans, or generations together with slaves, dependents or adopted strangers*

   (b) *a political division of the Roman people originally representing one of the three original tribes of ancient Rome*

2 *a group of persons having a common character, occupation, or interest*

3 *a category of taxonomic classification ranking below a subfamily; also: a natural group irrespective of taxonomic rank*

The Webster's authors have even defined the word "tribe" in terms that suited English-speaking people. If the authors had researched properly they would have found that in addition to the definitions they came up with, a tribe is a subdivision of an ethnic group (within a race) that is ruled by a chief within a kingdom. The existence of tribes even in America is evident in American Indian Society e.g. the Cherokee, Sioux or Crow Indian tribes. This tribal existence unfortunately was diluted and somewhat denied by the way these diverse groups of peoples were lumped together as "Red Indians", later acknowledged as "American Indians" and now "Native Americans".

Racial classification in Africa is integrated with the culture such that it determines how people live, get married to one another, govern, and respect each other. Tribal identities within the African race are so vital because quite apart from identification purposes, they are meant to prevent members of an extended family in a particular tribe from marrying into the same family.

There are no original racial classifications that were given to any race based on the complexion of their skin. The current racial classification that defines Africans as Black began with the colonization of Africa as European colonialists attempted to describe the skin color of the people concerned. As a result this negative practice was handed down.

The original racial classifications did indeed exist during the time the predecessors of the Webster's

Dictionary's authors were writing the dictionary; therefore, they should have consulted them, honored them and upheld them.

The racial and cultural differences that existed and still exist today in any country should not be forgotten. Each race should be well versed in its own culture and identity. When we ignore those identities, we are harmfully depriving that race of its right to identity. In a country like America where the majority is Caucasian, it is unfair for that majority to superimpose its racial views on the minority. That creates an unhealthy environment similar to what currently exists today. When the majority takes the position of protecting the minority's interests, it will create a harmonious atmosphere that is healthy for our society.

American society to an extent has tried to set a good example by creating social programs intended to help the minority. The different governing agencies have done this with the hope that these programs would work towards the betterment of the minority. However, in order for society to overcome the racial divide, we have to tackle the misconceptions and misrepresentations we are struggling with at the root.

The position that the authors of the Webster's Dictionary took may have been based on their educational background. The material from which the Webster's authors themselves were educated may have been written by people who had little regard for Africans. The programs such groups would implement may be against the cultural recommendations of the African race.

Just because a person has received formal education does not necessarily mean that he should impose the views he learned about in some books on another culture. Someone who did not care about respecting Africans and upholding their dignity may have written those books. His educational background may have been derived from sources that were insensitive to racial and social integration. We should consult the African people who know their community's cultural identity to guide us in any cultural or racial identification.

One way of evaluating the performance of agencies is to find out whether they teach or show wisdom in their work. This can be verified by the studies that they conduct on cultural activities and identifications. Today, when I see certain activities within our communities, I always ask the question: "What ever has happened to wisdom?

Chapter 7

I would like to emphasize the importance of educating ourselves about our race and racial identity. It is important for people to know what makes them what they are, based on their true racial identity. One race should not demoralize another by using negatively loaded racial names such as black, which has nothing to do with true racial classification. We have overlooked the impact that our basic understanding of race or misunderstanding of race has on racial relations in this society. Racial differences are real and can produce adverse racial reactions.

The American public was horrified to witness the desolation that the victims of Hurricane Katrina suffered in New Orleans, Louisiana in 2005. The slow response of federal relief efforts to the affected areas was attributed partly to the racial divide that exists in this country. Often in natural disasters, the hardest hit people are those that are less privileged. In American society, African-Americans fall under this category. It is true that other factors contributed to the lack of an adequate response to the victims. However, it was unfortunate that even in a time of emergency where the safety of human lives was concerned, racial differences affected relief efforts.

The African-American entertainer Kanye West sent shock waves around the nation when in a telethon to support the victims of Hurricane Katrina, he criticized President George W. Bush on national television for disregarding African-American people. He said, "George Bush don't like Black People". Certain members of the public considered his comments inappropriate. The real issue however was that the majority is often indifferent to the plight of the minority. This was confirmed on October 21st 2005 when Frances Townsend, President Bush's Homeland Security and Counter terrorism Advisor said, "The sense of everyone involved was that we were appropriately positioned and that we had the mechanisms in place. It turned out we were wrong, we had not adequately anticipated systemic and process and procedural problems that resulted in the failure." What is so frustrating to minorities like Kanye West is that it is hard to believe that (concerning the affected areas) senior government officials (who were charged to protect the population that died in Katrina) did not have the basic understanding that:

1. *New Orleans was built below sea level and thus had a potential to flood eventually.*
2. *The levees were built to resist category three hurricanes. Everyone knew days before hand what the strength of Katrina was and where it was headed.*
3. *A great percentage of the population was incapable of evacuating without government involvement.*

I cannot help but wonder in my spirit why the Mayor of New Orleans projected (before the bodies were recovered) that tens of thousands of people may have died in the floodwaters of Hurricane Katrina. I would hope that this was not true. We know that his projection was later disputed and that the death toll was recorded to be about a thousand two hundred and has been changing with time. How true is this number?

The authorities, in good faith had to give an account of the death toll to all the families that lost relatives to the hurricane. Not all of the bodies that were recovered could be positively identified. Given the fact that families were randomly evacuated to different cities and states in haste following the hurricane, it is possible for more than one family to believe that the same unidentified body was a member of their family in the absence of DNA testing.

Who can verify that the number of bodies recovered is the actual number of people that perished in the storm?

The city did not anticipate the devastation that was caused by the hurricane and the flooding that followed after the levees were broken. What did ninety percent of the population who were said to have had no transportation do when the city lacked an organized evacuation effort? Does this mean that only a thousand two hundred people lost their lives as confirmed by authorities? Of the mayor's projection and the confirmed death toll, which figure would represent more closely those who in reality lost their lives? Would all those who remain unaccounted for be placed within the smaller margin of the about one thousand two hundred bodies that were said to have been recovered?

Mr. William Bennet in September 2005 on his "Morning in America" radio show made remarks alluding to the fact that the abortion of African-American babies would decrease the crime rate in America. His exact comments were, " But I do know that it's true that if you wanted to reduce crime, you could, if that were your sole purpose, you could abort every black baby in this country and your crime rate would go down." It is true that his comments were based on a hypothesis. However, the very fact that he should make such a statement as a former Education Secretary under the Reagan administration and the author of "The Book of Virtues" is disturbing. It is these kinds of comments that lead the minority to doubt that officials in the capacity of Mr. Bennett (a former cabinet member) have their best interest at heart during disasters like Katrina. No wonder responsible politicians rebuked Bennett for his comments. We do not need such prejudicial remarks in our society.

It is however possible to overcome such prejudices to achieve an authentic integrated society. It was comforting to see Americans of different social and racial backgrounds later unite to assist the victims of Hurricane Katrina, whether through donations or volunteer support groups. There are many unreported humanitarian actions we may never hear about, such as people who spent their own money and used their own resources to help victims. Among them were people who were able to overcome previous prejudices when the situation called for it. There should be a willingness on everyone's part to overcome our prejudices and translate such togetherness into our everyday lives.

Racial misconceptions do not promote the integration of society. The O.J. Simpson trial was significant in exposing the racial divide in America. The trial highlighted the distrust that exists between African-Americans and Caucasians. The public's response was not based solely on whether or not Mr. Simpson was guilty of killing his ex-wife Nicole Brown Simpson and her friend. The very fact that the trial centered on an interracial couple was enough to create racial polarization in response to the trial. In addition, the trial raised questions about the inclusion of a Caucasian officer in the investigation who prior to the OJ Simpson case had made openly racist remarks that he did not like "Niggers" or "Mexicans".

We can minimize our distrust based on racial misconceptions by respecting each other and each other's culture. The willingness of America to solve its racial differences should be seen in how she continues to adapt to issues that are directly related to mutual racial harmony. We can start by using correct racial classifications and canceling insulting racial labels.

CHAPTER 8

Here are the answers to the issues that people raised to me before writing this book. I will be answering them in the order they were presented in Chapter One.

1. *If you are a descendant of Africa, it means you have African blood in you. Therefore, you are an African or African-American as the case may be. The key is to take the ancestral identities rather than the color of the skin. Descendants of Africans are Africans.*

2. *Any African-American that still calls himself Nigger needs to be educated regarding this. Informed people should not call themselves that*

way. There is no race called Nigger. It is an insult.

3. People who prefer to call themselves "Black" or "Black Americans" need to know that there is no race called "Black". Being African or African-American does have something to do with both their race and complexion. The description "African" has more to do with their ancestry, that is, where they are from originally, than their complexion alone. Their reservations about being connected to Africa do not change the fact that they originated from Africa.

4. Being American does not mean that your ancestors did not come from Africa. America (inclusive of all Americans) is made up of people from all over the world. These people had their own ways of living before they arrived on American soil. So "American" is the nationality for both the original natives and all those who settled here. Regarding discrimination, we should not overlook the fact that we were all created with a variety of complexions common to our geographical point

of origin. We did not choose these complexions. We were created that way. God created people of African origin darker skinned for a reason. One obvious reason is to protect them from the climatic conditions that they are exposed to in their places of origin. It is therefore unreasonable for any of us to look down upon another's complexion.

5. *Proper racial classification has great significance. It is especially important in African communities, for example, because it protects and preserves the identity and culture of parent families when couples get married.*

6. *One of the facts that most people need to realize is that African culture was and is structured in a way that the family remains connected. Many families got separated when the slave trade began and their racial classification was changed.*

Africans did not start the slave trade. It was a disaster that a lot of African people fought many losing battles trying to prevent. There are many events that took place that were not documented by the Europeans, but were passed along to generations of African children through oral bedtime stories and in family council meetings where older generations imparted to younger generations.

I do not know of any African who would deny or reject an African-American or a descendant of Africa for that matter. Even though I am from one part of Africa, my feelings and views are shared by many other Africans.

7. *People need to be educated about what the correct racial classification is. I am confident that the documents will eventually be changed to reflect true racial classifications rather than color or complexion.*

8. *"Colored" is not a race. People need to be educated about this as well.*

9. *"White" is not a race. It is a color. People that originate and formerly originated from Europe are Caucasians, Europeans or European–Americans. The term "White" was introduced*

by the Europeans and then later adopted by the Webster's Dictionary. Let me also say that this philosophy was passed down such that everybody now uses the term "White" for Caucasians as casually as they use "Black" for Africans and descendants of Africans.

Chapter 9

The second portion of this book will focus on crime. America has been suffering from a rising crime rate that is getting out of control. Everybody seems to be surprised and is wondering what to do about it. President Bill Clinton addressed it very vigorously when he was still in office. The current president George W. Bush is also addressing it with the help of the United States Congress and the Justice Department. This is an area that cannot be completely solved with the present policies that are being applied by government officials. If I were to be frank about it, I would say that crime explosion is inevitable considering the continuously favorable conditions that exist for it.

Let us tackle the crime issue by viewing it as a plant that has grown to maturity into a tree. It has roots, a trunk, branches, and leaves. We can take this illustration to represent a specific type of crime that we are analyzing. We should first identify the plant's feeding system such as the underground roots and the water and nutrients it draws from the ground.

The aboveground support systems must be identified too, such as air, sunlight and all the favorable and necessary weather conditions for its survival. All these support systems and favorable weather conditions will represent the conditions necessary for the occurrence and survival of crime. Let us visualize drawing a plant, labeling it as crime and marking in all the conditions necessary for its survival. Separate the easily identifiable conditions above ground from the less identifiable conditions underground.

After that, we can now start concentrating on how to control its growth and then how to actually kill the plant. The actions of controlling and killing the plant represent the actions of controlling and preventing crime. We can also say, the growth, control and killing of the plant will represent crime growth, crime control and crime prevention respectively. This is the most important part of solving the crime puzzle since it exposes what we are dealing with. The proper and accurate identification of these factors will become the foundation of a crime-fighting and crime-prevention policy in our homes, neighborhoods, cities, counties, states and countries.

Once we understand the concept of favorable and unfavorable conditions, we will understand better when we hear our government officials talk about the cooperation they need from us as private citizens in order to control crime in our cities. This understanding will also help us provide support based on the need and use of that support.

Why do authorities need cooperation from us? The tips we give authorities on possible crime rings in our vicinities and the vigilance of our neighborhood watch programs will eliminate any favorable conditions that may exist for the occurrence of crime.

Going back to my example, if the plant is to grow in any place at a particular spot, there must be favorable conditions there for it to grow. The same is true with crime. If our neighborhoods are plagued with crime, there are too many favorable conditions present for crime to occur and they need to be removed. If we do not water the plant, it will die. Likewise, if we do not provide favorable conditions for crime, it will not exist.

The environmental conditions, be they underground or above ground, will determine the growth process of a plant. The conditions necessary for crime to flourish can be analyzed in the same way.

If a child is fostered in an environment conducive to stealing, he could become a robber when he grows up. The home environment can force a child to learn how to be a criminal. Think about it for a minute. If you take a hungry child who is not well cared for, that child could steal food or money from wherever he can in order to eat. If the parents do not make sure the child eats right, that child will definitely start stealing in order to survive.

This could continue at school, where he cannot learn anything anyway because a child cannot learn while he is hungry. The chances that the child will become a dropout are overwhelming. When he drops out, chances are even slimmer that he will develop into a good citizen. He cannot meet the requirements necessary to live, let alone raise a good family. It may well be that by this time he may have been arrested, fathered a child or much worse. All this would have started at home, the primary place to be looked at if crime is to be prevented.

The home is the place where the seed is sown, good family values are taught, and good citizens are molded. It is the first place we need to look at for good citizen development lessons, which parents must provide.

Children are extensions of their families. They grow up to become what they are taught at home. For example, we cannot expect respect from a child who was never taught how to respect. We should therefore support good family values in the home if we want to prevent crime.

Note that a plant exists in a place when a seed is sown, a plant is transplanted or a part of one plant is grafted into another plant. By preventing the sowing of the seed, transplanting, and grafting one part of a plant into another plant, we can control the spreading of the plant. The same is true for crime.

The first stage of a child's life and even before the child is born is really the time to start creating an environment favorable for the prevention and control of crime. We should not wait until the child is grown up.

Criminals are children first. As babies they are all pure. Visit a maternity ward at a hospital to witness how evident that purity is. It makes you wonder why the world is so unfair with all the negative things it has in store for them. They will grow up to learn of murder, rape, prostitution, racism and so on.

We should instill preventative measures at the childhood stage rather than corrective measures later on. It may be too late.

Prevention is better than cure. The environment that a nation provides for all her children determines whether those children will become criminals or model, productive citizens.

The rate at which a nation can control crime will be determined by the rate at which she provides her babies anti-crime child development programs. What do I mean? Anti-crime policies, when developed into functional programs, will shield children as much as possible from criminal environments. The desired environments would have no criminal activity or influence on children to perform the criminal act itself.

If a child is placed in a crime-free environment and is discouraged from criminal activity, how will this child learn how to become something he or she is not accustomed to? A child learns about crime from the environment he or she grows up in. If you look at children's environments you will be amazed at what you will find out. Here are some examples:

1. *What kind of toys do we buy for or sell to our children? Visit any toy store and take a look around. Do we buy them toy guns, knives, war toys, violent video games or expose them to sexually explicit movies, games etc?*

2. *What kind of games do they play?*

3. *What kind of programs do they watch on television? How many of the cartoons they watch influence them towards criminal activity? Have we ever watched these cartoons from start to finish with our children?*

4. *How many children have been killed by the police while pointing toy guns at them? Why is it a legal and profitable practice to make and sell toy guns?*

Do you think you can stop it? If not, why? One way or another, America has to make a choice. We are creating criminals out of innocent children and hiding behind the dollars we profit from these acts. After that we blame them for what we made them to be. I have a different view from the current practices. First we have to change the policy on how children are induced to become criminals, starting with the items I have listed above.

First protect those who have not yet been exposed to crime through education and prevention. Then work on deterrent and corrective punishment programs for offenders. Do not make money from programs that teach children to become criminals. Rather than making money through avenues that could turn our children into criminals, why not make money out of the real criminals and use that money on healthy child development programs in order to break the cycle of crime?

In our states, do we know how much is budgeted annually towards crime related services? How much of that money is allocated to kindergarten and elementary schools to educate children against crime? The American people have to be willing to take some of the money that is being used to house criminals in prisons with all the amenities these prisons provide (i.e. recreational facilities, medical treatment etc), and use it for programs that would prevent children from becoming criminals.

The rate at which America is building prisons is alarming. The current number of prisons is not enough to hold inmates. Prisons and jails are overcrowded. The cost of prisons including their related support systems is unimaginable. There has to be a point when the public says, "Hell No! We cannot afford it." Questions need to be asked. Expenditures need to be evaluated. Here are some examples.

1. *Do we want to prevent the creation of criminals or do we just want to house them? If we house them, are we keeping them long enough till they have completed their sentences?*

2. *What is the actual cost of housing them? In other words, what is the total cost America is spending on criminals per year?*

3. *What is the breakdown of these expenditures?*

4. *How do prisoners spend their time in prison? Can that be improved?*

5. *What alternatives can we come up with?*

6. *Can the prisoners themselves build the prisons?*

7. *How much of the prisoners' work serves the public?*

8. *How many of the prisoners really want to live in prisons as opposed to those who regard prison as their only form of shelter?*

9. *Does the cost of housing a prisoner for one year equal the income earned by an average American?*

10. *Are you a victim of crime or do you know any victims?*

If you have pondered over the above, you should be saying, "Hell No to Crime!" A prison is meant to be a place where people are punished and reminded of the crime they committed so that they would not repeat it. A prison should be a place where you do not want to be, a place you would not want to return to.

If a prisoner is asked whether the crime he committed was worth it, he should be able to answer "No" without having to think twice about it. How many American prisoners can answer that?

Prisons should not be money guzzlers, but should be turned into money producers whose profits should be directed back into crime prevention programs that focus on children.

Can you think of ways that prisoners can give back to society? Make the system work for you rather than against you.

It does not make sense for government agencies to use tax dollars to pay for labor required in national disasters when we could use some prisoner assistance programs (while of course making provision for security concerns). We are already supporting the prison system with our tax dollars. We can cut down the additional cost of providing national services by using prison labor instead of paid contract laborers.

In what capacity can prisoners serve in dealing with natural disasters such as flooding, fires, mudslides and drought-stricken areas? In fire-prone areas, especially in the western states, why not use prisoners to make fireguards before the fires start? Why not use the services of prisoners to construct water canals to deliver water to desert areas?

Public Works Departments can use the services of prisoners to clean out rivers, bayous, ditches and water drains in cities in order to decrease the chances of flooding. Prison labor can also be used in the landscaping of city properties, or in maintaining interstate farm roads for example.

The only funds needed would be for the purchasing of equipment. Meanwhile, we would preserve prison space and double the prison occupancy by providing twelve-hour work shifts that would provide the general public with protective services from natural disasters.

By wisely planning before disasters strike, we can save a lot of tax dollars to use on the front end of child development and crime prevention programs.

Programs that can make prison systems self-supportive should be implemented to cut costs. Rather than spending money on prisoners, why not put them to work so that they can support themselves? Why pay them to pump weights so that when they come out of prison they are invigorated to carry out further negative exploits since they would be physically stronger than when they first went in?

Preventive programs should be implemented to deter crime. Some criminals may change after exposure to rigid policies. If the following policies are implemented, we would solve the case of the potential or even the habitual criminal.

Fines and bail moneys should go to the victims. The government should not make money out of the losses the victims suffer without granting the victims the right to collect a portion of the fines imposed at judgment. The government can then deliver the monies to the victims upon payment so that there is no contact between the victims and the perpetrators. Let me state here that no amount of money can nullify the suffering of the victims. I believe however that this practice would provide a greater deterrent from criminal activity than what we have at present.

Criminals should be penalized based on the crimes they commit to recover the financial losses the victims suffer. Each offense would carry a fine that raises funds to compensate the victims in addition to serving a prison sentence. This would be like taxing a smoker out of smoking. Their income can support victims and victims' families and fund deterrent programs in schools and the private sector like community youth centers, for example.

The money raised should be directed at programs to teach children about the disadvantages of crime. If the bulk of the earnings of criminals is given to the victims and also applied towards crime preventive programs, there would be less crime today.

Anyone who has the ability to plan, think and execute a crime definitely has the ability to understand the gravity of the punishment that should follow. That person should be made to believe that crime does not pay. If this is understood there would be less crime and more respect for the law. America should create more effective crime deterrent programs.

There is a need for more discipline within families. Governmental laws must free parents from prosecution when they administer discipline, so long as they do not abuse their children. Authorities should not close their eyes on child abuse. They should still keep their eyes open for child abuse. Agencies against child abuse should not however create problems where they do not exist.

If my father did not discipline me when I ran away from school in my early years of education, I would not be writing this book. By remembering that criminal activity more often than not originates from the home environment, authorities must strengthen the family unit and provide the support needed for parents to instill discipline. Discipline is lost when parents fear prosecution. Therefore the children plainly do what they want, forever expecting life to bend to their demands. This attitude may induce later criminal activity.

If parents felt free to control their children, most children would follow the desires of their parents. No parent wishes for his child to become a criminal. Parents want to protect their children from harm and bring them up to be responsible citizens. The problem is that a lot of them cannot afford to provide the environment necessary to protect the children. This is the revelation that America needs to embrace in order to put a dent in the crime rate.

Let us make it affordable for parents to raise their children in the right environments, educate them adequately, and teach them the ways of wisdom in becoming good, model citizens. We must be conscious of what we provide children. Remember that children learn what we teach them. It should not be a crime to instill necessary discipline in a child.

Chapter 10

The inscription on American currency, "In God We Trust" is becoming a forgotten emblem. The American founding fathers adopted this acknowledgement of their belief system as the foundation on which they built this nation. Why must America today forsake the very foundation on which she was built? Why are we stamping God out of the very fabric of American society?

The forefathers who initiated the inscription were correct in trusting God as the center and foundation of American society. They understood the implications of that principle. Is it a wonder that America is the most prosperous and most powerful nation in the world today?

Why is today's society now erasing this principle from public life and in schools? Why are we so bent on banning the freedom of religious expression in schools? Has the crime rate not catapulted ever since prayer was banned from schools? Why is there such a vicious attack on the display of the Ten Commandments? The display of a moral code should be viewed more as an avenue for building good character than an infringement on people's liberties. Schools should be places that respect the moral values which the family unit instills in its children.

If children cannot freely exercise their religious beliefs at school, beliefs that are not harmful in anyway but build good moral character, what kind of school environment are we creating for them? Are we surprised that we are now threatened with incidents like the Columbine High School shootings, to the extent that parents are now concerned about the safety of their children when they send them off to school? Schools should respect and uphold the basic foundations that made this country what it is and still make it what it is today. The basic foundations are those the forefathers built this country on, which they expressed in the words "In God We Trust".

Since we are not abiding by the foundational principles, we now have a rising issue of juvenile crime. The battle to control juvenile crime should begin at home. The family structure should be set up in a way that builds sound moral character in a child. Such character building can shield a child from adopting bad habits when he later interacts with the public. The cost of preventing crime on the family level is much less than trying to deal with it later. Parents must be involved. They cannot depend on law enforcement to keep their children in check. Parents must monitor the whereabouts of their children at all times. They should constantly address the following questions:

1. *Which negative traits does our child portray?*

2. *Does he steal from us?*

3. *Does he beat up on his siblings?*

4. *Does our child have a temper?*

5. *What does our child do at school?*

6. *What kind of friends does our child play with?*

7. *Do the friends come from good families?*

8. *Are those families made up of good citizens? Do they recklessly drink alcohol, do drugs or have bad habits the child can pick up?*

9. *Are those families racist or prejudiced?*

10. *Do we spend quality time with our child?*

11. *Do we talk to our child, laugh and cry or sing together?*

12. *Do we really know our child?*

13. *Which values can we instill in our child to ensure that he develops into a good citizen?*

Imagine what type of environment we could have if a community of people would stop to ask themselves these questions. If every community addresses these questions, we all can build communities that foster good children and not juvenile delinquents.

As I stated earlier, no parent wishes for his child to become a criminal. If parents are well equipped to bring up their children right, America will start seeing the juvenile crime rate decrease. Just imagine what type of environment there would be if a whole community had people who would ask themselves these kinds of questions. If these can be asked on a community wide basis, we can have communities that are capable of controlling and caring for their children. The key is for the federal, state, and local governments to consider the juvenile crime rate as a national disaster in order to implement the programs that I have pointed out.

CHAPTER 11

We cannot talk about eliminating crime without acknowledging that racial classifications do have an impact on crime. Once we have been able to do that, we can address key areas like racially related and racially motivated crimes. Have you ever wondered why American prisons are filled with a disproportionate racial representation of prisoners?

On October 04, 2005 on news.yahoo.com/s/usatoday on the internet, DeWayne Wickam wrote, "Of the men and women behind bars last year, 910,200 were African-American, 777,500 were Caucasian and

395,400 were Hispanic, according to the Bureau of Justice Statistics."

Is it that African-Americans commit more crime? How many of minority prisoners are in prisons based on wrong convictions? Why is it that the minority as a whole is filling up the prisons and jails? Several professionals have attempted to address these questions, but have not been able to effect change to the needed extent.

In the Houston Police Department DNA crime lab, mistakes, some of which led to the wrongful conviction of innocent prisoners, were detected. Authorities had to ask for the suspension of executions of death row prisoners who where convicted on evidence from that laboratory. Subsequently, the review of the evidence used to convict some of the prisoners led to their freedom, thank God!

Has anyone ever thought of studying racial relations and their impact on prison and jail populations? The statistics gathered by the FBI on arrests made from 1999 through 2003 show that more Caucasians were arrested than African-Americans in each of those years.

America, as everybody knows, is made up of the descendants of multiple races with their respective original multiracial cultures. In good faith she has tried to fuse all the different racial cultures into one national American culture. Usually with such integration, the majority tries to impose its culture on the minority, again in good faith.

When a race tries to acknowledge its culture, other cultural groups may have reservations about the practices being performed. These reservations stem from the misinterpretation of cultural activities and the cultural meanings of practices that a group may uphold.

Misunderstanding of cultural practices may even occur within the same racial group. This is because fellow members may not be well versed in their own cultural practices. These divisions may be expressed in acts of unnecessary violence.

America needs to understand first the concept of cultural existence, which encompasses racial and cultural differences. If America understands this, most racially related crimes can be eliminated. This realization would expose the existent misunderstandings I mentioned above.

Understanding and acceptance would help build tolerance for existing differences in order to reach a common ground. There is nothing wrong with the existence of cultural and racial differences. These differences are not there by choice. We inherited them from our ancestors. We need to be wise however, in how we interpret and use them in order to achieve social harmony.

When people are celebrating their culture, we should not automatically write off their practices as radical and offensive. Celebrating culture, at least from the African and African-American point of view, is a way of passing along or teaching African wisdom to the younger generations.

This kind of wisdom is not taught in schools. These celebrations reinforce cultural identity thereby encouraging appreciation, understanding and respect for the history and practices of that group. This gives the children a foundation on which to build their lives.

Not all African cultural practices resemble what we see on the Discovery Channel or in Tarzan movies that most Americans see on their television screens. Most are moderate, positive practices, which give people a sense of being. These practices are not for the purpose of reorganizing any militant attitudes, as Western literature portrays. Taking away a person's cultural identity is like trying to disrupt the flow of a river. A river must regain its natural flow. It must follow its own course.

Is it not better to encourage leadership by allowing them to direct people within their natural flow, as opposed to denouncing positive identity images that they may try to build? I am often surprised to hear negative commentaries about African-African leaders who try to lead people into their cultural identity.

Many African-American children have no positive images of their African ancestry. They barely even have positives images of their African-American ancestry. I do not have any doubt that most African-American children that end up in gangs do so because they have no positive role models to emulate.

Some of them commit crimes in the name of being "Black" and claim to be taking back what is rightfully theirs due to the losses they suffered on the account of slavery. They use slavery as an excuse to justify their actions. They have not been taught or given positive cultural goals to live up to. It is in the absence of the right cultural goals that they are led into gangs where their energies are misdirected into criminal activity.

Encouraging leadership would therefore help to control the crime rate by channeling such negative energy into positive, constructive energy. The input of external leadership in molding our youth is very much needed. However, as mentioned earlier, the family unit is primarily responsible for instilling the right cultural goals in children.

Cultural expression is not always welcome when it is delivered in a different package than expected. A perfect example is the initial response to rap music when it first came about. Rap music was misunderstood and prejudged to be gang music because it was different from the more familiar and more accepted types of African-American music like Rhythm and Blues, for example.

African-American people throughout their history have relied on music as a means of encouraging and expressing themselves. Yet their evolving cultural expression in the arena of music was met with distrust. Rap music, at its inception, was mainly an expression of the experiences of the songwriters, as most music is.

Eventually, rap music became more widely accepted and grew into one of the most popular types of music today.

We should however not be so blinded by the misrepresentation of culture, especially when crime is committed in the name of cultural identity. This does not only hurt relations within the group in which it occurs. It also hurts external relations with other groups.

The misrepresentation and misinterpretation of cultural identity heightens distrust between different racial groups. In this case, internal policing is essential and should precede external involvement. Internal policing within the group would go a long way to prevent tensions that arise from prejudices that come with external policing.

Premature external policing occurs because of misunderstanding and misinterpretation of cultural traditions. In the past, such misinterpretation has led to the imprisonment of so many innocent people. Many innocent African-American youth have been swept up in police raids aimed at gangsters because they were at the wrong place at the wrong time. They may have innocently attended a function in which gang members were present. When violent activity took place and law enforcement was called in, they were included with the guilty by reason of association, when such association did not exist.

This all boils down to the distrust that stems from racial and cultural differences. The innocent do not have to end up in jail or prison. They must not share the same fate as the guilty. On the other hand, the gang members could have been spared from their predicament provided they had a clear understanding of their cultural identity to steer them away from criminal activity. They would not suffer this predicament if there had been anti-crime child development programs (which I suggested earlier) to direct them away from such negative environments. We should learn to embrace our cultural differences in order to create harmony between ourselves.

Before I conclude, I would like to extend my thanks to the following people and groups. They have made it possible for me to write today. They are:

1. *God, for creating all of us and giving us the ability to think and live the way we do today with all the blessings we all take for granted.*

2. *My parents who raised me to be the person that I am, considering the conditions of colonialism they lived with.*

3. *The Ledgerwood and Smith families who were my first American families. They made me part of their families in a way I did not expect. They were so different from the colonial rulers I had left in Africa who were holding my father as a political prisoner. I do miss them, and love them.*

4. *The African-American communities for forming civil rights organizations like the NAACP, Urban League, the Rainbow PUSH Coalition and all the other groups that have positively changed the lives of people and the way they are governed. They have taken positive steps to address racial indifferences*

and create a better living environment for people of all races. They continuously pave the way to a better living environment for us all.

Lastly, I want to extend my thanks to the forgotten people. These are all the people who no one seems to think about, mainly because they died without trace. They are the families who did not know what hit them when they fell to their deaths. They are the people who tried to stop the slave trade. They fought battles and lost. They are the people that died in one way or the other resisting slavery in Africa, on ships in the Caribbean, in the Americas and in Europe. They are the people that were killed by the jaws of the slave trade. They are my people. We honor them. We love them. We miss them. We will never forget them. We will remember.

May their sacrifices resound through the ages. Amen.

CHAPTER 12

The following is a list of African names from Zimbabwe that I put together as a token or bonus to some of you who may want them. There are many people that have asked for African names to name their children with. If you are interested, I do encourage you to ask Africans in your area for other African names, since there are many African languages. The best way would be to visit the continent. If you have any African friends you can ask them to connect you with members of their families. They would love to have you. Most Africans are very generous, courteous, hospitable and gracious.

MALE NAMES   DEFINITION

Male Name	Definition
Simba	Strength
Mapfumo	Spears
Tapfuma	We are rich
Tapfumaneyi	What are we rich of?
Simbisayi	Strengthen
Nembiri	With fame
Shingai	Be brave
Masiyiwa	You have been left
Mudavunhu	A lover of people
Musindo	Troublesome
Mutize	One who runs away
Tambeneyenyu	Play with your own
Pauro/Paurosi	Paul
Timoti	Timothy
Mutamba	One who plays
Taremeredwza	We have been honored
Tatenda	We are thankful

FEMALE NAMES   DEFINITION

Female Name	Definition
Tsitsi	Grace/Mercy
Itayi/Itai	Do something
Mutsa	Grace/Mercy
Nomusa/Momutsa	With Grace
Anesu	God is with us
Danai/Danayi	Love each other
Rudo	Love
Nyasha	Mercy
Sekayi/Sekesayi	Laugh/Make them laugh
Chenayi	Be clean
Chenasayi	Be extra clean
Mwoyochena	A clean heart
Netsayi	Be troublesome
Ruse	Ruth
Sipiwe	We were given

Zvipo .... Gifts
Tandiwe/Mudiwa .... The loved one
Rudairo .... Faith
Sibongile .... We are thankful
Chengetayi .... Protect

MALE/FEMALE NAMES   DEFINITION

Batsirai/Batsi .... You help /Help
Yamurai/Yamu .... You help/Help
Kudzai/Kudza .... Respect
Fungai/Funga .... Think
Bongai .... Thank (Thank God)
Tendai .... Thank
Tsikai/Tsika .... Step on
Kumbirayi .... Ask
Karirayi .... Hope
Zvikomborero .... Blessings
Tinoenda .... We go
Tichaenda .... We will go
Farayi/Farai .... Be happy
Nangisayi .... Look
Chipo .... A gift
Chido .... Beloved

www.ingramcontent.com/pod-product-compliance
Lightning Source LLC
Chambersburg PA
CBHW020300290526
45784CB00003B/1308